Sugar Cravings:

How to Stop Sugar Addiction & Lose Weight

Anthea Peries

If you enjoyed reading this book,
please leave a positive review on
Amazon. The author would
appreciate it.

Thanks!

Disclaimer Notice:

CHAPTER 1

Introduction

In this book, I am going to tell you about the problem with sugar, why too much sugar is bad for you, sugar addiction and cravings, how you can break the cycle and the benefits involved for you to reduce your sugar intake, plus lots more including recipe ideas to keep sugar help withdrawal, your goals, managing emotional eating, information about alternative therapies, weight loss plus more.

Don't wait any longer, think about your health; read this book and start to conquer your sugar cravings and addiction today.

There is no secret about Governments around the world beginning to clamp down on sugar. They are beginning to pass taxes on the likes of sugary snacks and drinks, barring them from all kinds of organizations and institutions such as schools, and there are even more treatment programs open to the public who think that they are addicted to sugar. What is the actual truth of the matter? Is it that sugar has become the new enemy?

Types of Sugar

For centuries Coca leaves were used in their regular state to grind, chew on or make tea. This seemed to be a normal thing to do and there were apparently no issues surrounding this. However, coca became highly processed and transformed into a hazardous and addictive remedy or drug known as cocaine.

You may recall that the poppy flower seemed to have suffered the exact same fate. This used to be an effective and safe tea, which was very often drunk for relaxation purposes and for pain; again, this also became so highly-processed that it became a dangerous and powerful, addictive opiate.

Some of you may know that sugar initially starts out as sugar cane, which is a healthy plant. If consumed in its organic form you cannot eat enough of it to make you ill. But when it is highly concentrated and processed it can become just a drug. Using lab rats, sugar outdone cocaine as a preference.

One needs to be aware that there are various kinds of sugar, some are natural and some super processed - to the extent that even if they started out organically, they are not organic or natural.

- **Fructose** – Do not get muddled by the word. While fructose comes from fruit, it has still gone through enough processing that it becomes a highly-concentrated form of sugar. To be fair to people this type of fructose really should be labelled "industrial fructose". Eating reasonable amounts of fructose made from natural fruit is not dangerous and should not be avoided. But when it is processed, it transforms into something else entirely and can cause health problems.

- **Glucose** – This type of sugar is already in your blood. You find it in natural plant foods like vegetables, fruits, and carbohydrates, particularly in starchy foods. It is one of the most significant medications and naturally available in nature. Glucose supplies most of the energy to your brain and it is fundamental for numerous functions such as metabolic health, respiration and much more. So if you wish to be able to focus and to think clearly, you need to have the right amount of glucose. Of course glucose is created industrially by using starchy plants like wheat, rice, corn, and other ingredients too.

- **Lactose** – this is found in milk and made from galactose and glucose. Industrially it is formed as a by-product of the dairy industry. The majority of humans produce their own lactase to digest this type of sugar far into adulthood. However, there are some people, particularly from eastern and south-eastern Asia and also parts of Africa that cannot properly digest this type of sugar in adulthood.

- **Maltose** – This type of sugar found in the germination process when the seeds break down their starch stores for the food to sprout and propagate. This kind of sugar can result in many types of intolerances besides kidney stones, weight gain and more. However, eating it in its organic state such as in sweet potatoes, barley, soybeans, and in wheat (besides those sufferers of celiac), can be healthy.

- **Sucrose** – This type of sugar is from beets and cane. Processing can give the appearance of table sugar. Prior to processing it has many health benefits, minerals and vitamins. Tasty honey is mainly fructose and glucose and has trace amounts of sucrose.

So now you know how the majority of sugars begin in a natural state and are not bad in their organic and most whole form that is until they undergo high levels of processing. It is the super-processing that makes it bad for you, because it transforms any natural sugars into highly addictive drug-like substances.

CHAPTER 2

13 Reasons Sugar Is Bad for You

So what are the reasons sugar is thought to be bad for you? It has been said that sugar is one of the worst things you can consume, even more than fat.

1. **The Immune System** – If you eat too much processed sugar this reduces your ability to ward off and to kill germs inside your body. It only takes a little to do this. Only two sugar drinks would stop your capacity to fight off a flu bug and lead to failing health. This would not mean that you should not get vaccines if you don't consume any sugar, however when it comes to health, including dental health, eliminating added sugar will boost your immunity exponentially.

2. **Mineral Balance** – If you suffer from insomnia at night, or are constipated and having other issues, you may be having problems with your mineral balance. If you eat a lot of sugar, this will deplete your magnesium stores to process it. Plus, you can lose chromium through your urine if you eat plenty of sugar.

3. **Behavior Problems** – Sugar and the lack of sugar can affect a child's behavior in several ways. If a child feels hungry and their blood sugar is down, they will become drowsy and grumpy. If a child has too much sugar, they can become agitated and hyper active or energetic. The key to healthier behavior is blood sugar balance.

4. **Empty Calories** –Processed sugar has no health benefits whatsoever and therefore, when you eat any sugary meals, you are basically eating empty wasted calories that

will only cause you to gain weight. What is more, the fact that sugar is very often mixed with fat and salt will only make the effects even worse. So it's far better to avoid the added sugar whenever you can.

5. **Elevated Insulin Responses** – When insulin responds in a healthy way, your cells will release the exact level of insulin you need in the body. But, when you eat too much sugar on a regular basis, particularly in "overdose" quantities, your body, then becomes very confused about when it needs to release insulin and when not to do so.

6. **Damages Cells and Tissues** – The tissue in your eyes, nerves and kidneys, etc., carry more sugar than other organs. This means that the body can become more damaged from residual sugar

because it starts to damage the smaller blood vessels.

7. **Causes High Blood Triglyceride Levels** – There appear to be no known symptoms for high blood triglyceride levels so it is best to get a blood test to find out how high it is. This is usually part of your overall cholesterol test.

8. **Contributes to Hyperactivity** – Studies have shown both results in that sugar does cause hyperactivity and sugar doesn't cause it. Remember that any drug can affect humans either way. You cannot ignore the possibility of either outcome as parents often report problems with hyperactivity in their child after consuming too much sugar.

9. **Anxiety** – Processed or refined sugars enter the blood stream faster, and leave the

blood stream quickly. This progression can cause more anxiety overall. People who are addicted to sugar often eat to suppress anxiety so this makes the problem even worse. It's best to eliminate any added sugars to begin with.

10. **Poor Concentration** – the reason sugar affects concentration is mainly because of the fast speed by which processed sugar invades and then leaves our blood cells. You have to have consistent and balanced levels of glucose to supply your brain, not short bursts of sugar like soft drinks, bar of chocolate or sugary cereal.

11. **Feeds Some Cancers** – Cancer cells love sugar because, like most living things they need the sugar to spread and to grow. Cancer cells love white sugar, white flour, and high fructose corn syrup. The good news is that if

you decrease your consumption of processed sugar, cutting down your cancer risks.

12. **Hypoglycemia** – Low blood sugar occurs in people who have hypoglycemia. This is a condition on its own, but also happens in people who have diabetes and use medications like insulin because their bodies cannot produce enough on their own.

13. **Poor Digestion** – Processed sugar is acidic, so the more alkaline you have in your body, the healthier you will become. If your stomach is acidic, you'll suffer from heartburn, GERD, and many other digestive issues.

Every person can get affected in different ways. It's best to monitor your own symptoms and health problems and if you have any of these issues, try avoiding processed sugar first and see if you notice any changes in your own health.

The Surprising Places Sugar Hides

In this chapter, I am going to tell you about hidden sugars.

Most hidden sugars in our diets today is often very hard to find. You'll be amazed at the things that are added and unnecessary.

- **Breakfast Cereal** – Sugar in sugary cereal the hidden sugar in so-called healthy cereals, some "healthy" cereals have more than 23 grams of sugar per serving.

- **Asian Food** – Most restaurants - made or packaged Asian food has a large amount of sugar in it. Even sushi and the way you make sushi rice include adding sugar to it. You can make your own Asian food at home to ensure that the sugar level is not too high.

- **Canned and Packaged Soups and Sauces** – Thankfully, we can check the labels. Some low fat yogurts have more than 15 grams of sugar. Even spaghetti sauce and gravy have more sugar than a sugary soda drink. If you want to be sure to eat less sugar, read labels and find no-sugar options or better still is to make your own.

- **Frozen Yogurt** – Just because you read the word yogurt doesn't mean it's healthy. It's as sugary as regular ice-cream. It's still a dessert, so treat it as if it's a dessert. Don't have it for a meal, and don't you believe you're eating healthier either. If you prefer real ice cream for a sugary snack you are free to eat that instead, because one is not better than the other, when it comes down to sugar.

- **Smoothies** – Yes, they're all the rage these days aren't they? And there are smoothie shops banking on it. But, most smoothie shops use fruit with added sugar which removes any benefits you would have from drinking a smoothie at all. If you make your own, watch it when recipes ask for dried fruit too. Using whole, fresh fruit is much better.

- **Bread** – Although some bread that is good for you, most bread is made with very refined flour and sugar. Both affect blood sugar and wheat bread may be high in sugar, so read the labels. Bread which is normally low in sugar is rye or spelt. Remember, you can make your own bread to avoid additives and hidden sugars that can harm your health.

- **Condiments** – We often like to dip everything in something. But, if you dip your fresh fruit or celery into the wrong thing, you could make matters worse. Instead, make your own condiments or read the labels carefully.

Today there are so many low-sugar varieties of condiments, including low-sugar ketchup around.

- **Canned Beans** – Again, check the labels on canned beans, particularly the ones with any type of sauce on them such as chili or baked beans. These are usually very high in sugar that if you compared it to a cake you would not know which was which by the amount of sugar!

- **Muffins** – Yes, muffins are high in sugar, but even the ones that sound healthy are cakes in muffin form with a healthy flour or healthy name added. So don't be fooled, they are all high in sugar. There are some recipes for low-sugar muffins, though; searching the internet and you will find them.

- **Yogurt** – Did you know that frozen yogurt can be high in sugar, so is most sweetened yogurt – especially low-fat yogurts. The best way to combat this problem is to make your own yogurt or eat yogurt as a dessert. You can buy plain yogurt and add your own fruit and stevia to create a low-sugar snack that is healthy due to the probiotics in yogurt.

Note that anything pre-made and packaged has a tendency of too much sugar. It's best to read the labels and decide for yourself. Keep in mind that the average adult should not consume more than 90 grams, or 5 percent of their total calories, in excess sugar on a daily basis.

How Much Sugar Is Too Much?

In this chapter, I am going to tell you about the amount of sugar involved in all of this.

One thing that needs to be made clear is that there is a difference from naturally occurring sugars and added sugar. There is sugar in all plant food and we know plant food is good for you. In fact, most of your plate should make up plant food if you really want to be at your peak health.

So, breaking this down, adults should not ingest more than about 90 grams in total of all sugars each day. How much of that is added sugar depends on your ideal daily caloric intake.

That means if you eat 1500 calories each day, you can eat 90 grams of sugar a day. How much of that you want to be processed and added sugar is up to you. But obviously, keeping the quantity of added sugar much lower is far better for your health. This gives you some room to experiment with your health and to have a fun on special occasions.

When you consider that a cup of grapes has around 15 grams of sugar, but a can of soda pop has 39 grams, it can make the choice for you much easier to make. Amazing isn't it? If you really want a drink, you can try a sugar-free Zevia or even better, LaCroix. But a tall glass of filtered water with a cup of grapes will fill you up longer. The main thing you need to do is to find substitutes that you truly enjoy and like, while not overshooting the 90 grams of sugar allowance you have for each day.

The more natural sugars that you consume within that 90 grams, the better you will feel. And there are so many low glycemic choices that you can make.

Fruit

Apples – 1 small = 15g
Apricots – 1 cup = 15g
Banana – 1 medium = 14g
Blackberries – 1 cup whole = 7g
Blueberries – 1 cup whole = 15g
Cantaloupe – 1 cup diced = 12g
Cranberries – 1 cup whole = 4g
Grapefruit – 1 cup = 16g
Guavas – 1 cup = 15g
Honeydew – 1 cup diced = 14g
Lemons – 1 wedge = 0.2g
Limes - 1 wedge = 0.15g
Papaya – 1 cup 1" cubed = 11g
Peaches – 1 cup sliced = 13g
Raspberries – 1 cup whole = 5g
Rhubarb – 1 cup diced = 1.3g
Strawberries – 1 cup whole = 7g
Tomatoes – 1 large whole = 4.8g
Watermelon – 1 cup diced = 9g

Vegetables

Artichokes – 1 large = 1.6g
Asparagus – 1 cup = 2.5g
Broccoli – 1 cup chopped = 1.5g
Carrots – 1 medium = 2.9g
Celery – 1 cup chopped = 1.8g
Corn – 1 cup = 1.1g
Cucumber – 1 8-in = 5g
Green Beans – 1 cup = 3.3g
Kale – 1 cup chopped = 1.6g
Lettuce – 1 head = 2.8g
Soybean sprouts – 1 cup = 0.1g
Spinach – 1 cup = 0.1g
Summer squash – 1 cup sliced = 2.5g
Swiss chard – 1 cup = 0.4g

As you may see, the majority of natural foods doesn't have "too much" sugar. If you can eat 90 grams of sugar a day and you choose wisely from the lower sugar fruits and veggies, you'll be amazed at how much you can eat if you just avoid the added sugars. When you consider that one teaspoon of processed sugar is 4.2 grams, you can decide what is best to eat in every given situation.

CHAPTER 3

Are You Addicted to Sugar?

As you read this book, do you start thinking about ways to combat the 90-gram maximum of sugar that you can have each day? Remember that the 90 grams of sugar (per UK government guidelines) intake per day have nothing to do with how many carbohydrates you eat each day. This is a separate number that you should keep track of.

What Causes Sugar Addiction?

Overwhelming sugar cravings have shown in research that you can actually become hooked on it. Scientists have discovered that sugar is addictive and it stimulates the exact same pleasure centers of the brain as does heroin and cocaine.

How can you break the sugar addiction?

Eliminate processed foods....

Boost your serotonin by getting exercise....

Satisfy your sweet tooth naturally with organic foods. ...

Drink plenty of water....

Keep your blood sugar stable and avoid sugary snacks....

Have plenty of fresh greens....

Consume more sea vegetables...

Common behaviors that can predict sugar addition:

- **You Eat Too Much** – If you love certain foods that you can't get enough of; imagine they're likely to be high in sugar. Sugar doesn't make you satisfied, so it's hard to stop. This is often worsened if sugar is combined with fat and sodium. For example, you may be eating donuts which are also high in salt and fat, but would you eat them without the sugar? I doubt it.

- **You Crave Processed Carbohydrates** – If you're habitually craving refined carbs like potato chips, crackers, and bread, you may have a problem with sugar too. Often, excluding added sugars can reduce cravings that you're having for highly processed carbohydrates over a period of time.

- **You Crave Salty Foods** – Alongside processed foods,

salt and sugar seem to go well together. If you feel like you could lick a pretzel or suck a peanut and be happy, you may be addicted to sugar. Look at the amount of sugar in the snacks you normally eat. If super processed, you can bet they have too much added sugar.

- **You Crave Meat** – This may sound strange, but if you desire meat when you really don't need it and aren't that hungry, you could be craving the spices often on meat such as BBQ sauce which is very high in sugar.

- **Every Meal Is High in Sugar** – Do you find that your typical meal is higher in sugar than it ought to be? Keep in mind that the maximum of 90 grams is a maximum. That doesn't mean you need to eat that much sugar in a day either. If you feel ill and aren't very healthy, you can reduce that amount down. The best way to do that is to totally avoid any extra sugars and only eat the sugar that is naturally in plants.

- **You Get Moody without Sugar** – If you are feeling grumpy and moody, the problem could be the sugar amount. If you often suffer lows and highs in blood sugar, when you have a dip, you will suffer from grumpy moods. This can be intensified by eating sugary things like candy, which will provide a fast spike and also a quick dip too.

- **You Feel Powerless Over Sugar** – Do you sometimes feel like you don't want to eat that sugary snack, yet you eat it anyway because you think it'll make you feel better? This is common in people who work long days; particularly students. It's true that eating a feel good, sugary snack will temporarily help, merely you'd feel far better eating fruit with natural sugars and fiber to help slow down the sugar concentration.

- **You start and End Your Day with Sugar** – Look at your day, what do you eat for breakfast? What do you eat before going to bed? What is the first and last thing you eat every day? If you're eating sugar both in the morning and at night, particularly added processed sugar and not sugar in whole plants, it is a sign that you could have an addiction to sugar.

- **You Suffer a 3 PM Slump** – If you work in an office, you'll notice this lot more than if you are retired or work from home. But pay attention if somewhere after lunch you start falling asleep while you're working or feel as if you need a nap. Look at your diet. Are you giving yourself energy for lunch or are you setting yourself up for a sugar crash?

If you are going through any of these problems, it is a good idea to calculate how much sugar you eat on a daily basis. The majority of people consume double the sugar intake maximum of 90 grams a day, due to hidden, added and processed sugars.

CHAPTER 4

Tips on Breaking Your Sugar Habit

The good news is that you don't need to work too hard to break a sugar addiction unless you aim for zero sugar and that would not be very healthy as you know. Instead, first aim for a reduction, and then you can eliminate more and more gradually with good food choices.

- **Avoid Processed Food** – When it comes to sugar in food, the biggest culprit is processed food. Processed food has lots of sugar, and not then, it has plenty of chemicals. Avoiding processed food can eliminate almost all of the added sugar you are eating.

- **Get Plenty of Sunshine** – Strange as it may seem, one reason people like to eat sugar is serotonin, this is the feel-good hormone. When you eat plenty of sugar, you achieve a spike in serotonin. And yes, you get a severe crash too. There are far better ways to increase serotonin levels; one is the sunshine, when the sun shines of course. You also get vitamin D which will improve your mood.

- **Get Plenty of Sleep** – If you have trouble sleeping, then you need to find out why. Avoid sugars, caffeine, and anything that is stimulating you several hours before bed. You should go to sleep on an empty stomach for a better sleep, but this is hard for some people.

- **Drink Enough Water** – Staying hydrated is most important in order to avoid cravings in general, including sugar cravings. When we become born, we have the perfect thirst detector. But, life very often causes us to ignore our bodies' signals.

Therefore, measure the amount of water you drink each day to ensure that you're drinking a minimum of 64 ounces to 100 ounces of water a day, depends on your body weight.

- **Focus on Stability** – Try to keep your sugar balanced. To do this, have regular meal times. For some, that may mean up to six meals a day; for others, the traditional three meals a day is enough. It depends on what suits you. Eat when you feel real hunger pangs.

- **Eat Your Greens** – Have you not noticed when you eat more greens like spinach, turnip greens, kale, and so forth, your sugar cravings diminish or go away? So, when you get the craving, try eating a bowl of freshly steamed spinach with good red wine vinegar splashed on it, and your cravings may well disappear.

- **Incorporate Fermented Foods and Drinks** – Not only do they keep your stomach acid and bacteria balanced, fermented foods and drinks are great sweet tooth killers. Buy prepared fermented foods or you can make your own. Remember though that a tiny amount of sugar is used in the fermentation process, but that is fine.

- **Meditate** – On occasion, sugar cravings are a sign that you need to simply slow down and get centered. Stress plays a big role in appetite and sugar cravings. So take the time to meditate, up to 10 minutes per day. If you don't wish to meditate, just pray or sit silently and relax, this can work too.

Integrating these tips on a daily basis makes a big difference when you're trying to cut down sugar cravings and break the sugar habit. It's not

going to happen overnight either, so
be patient and focus on adding in
good foods to your life rather than on
what you are avoiding or eliminating.

How to Fight Sugar Addiction Withdrawal Symptoms

When you first decide to eliminate added sugar from your diet, you will experience withdrawal symptoms – particularly your sugary treats including caffeine if you decide to give that up too. You don't want to substitute sugar with chemical things, so it's better to try to get over each of the symptoms you may have.

- **Depression** – If you ever notice after giving up added sugar, you are feeling down and depressed, try to ensure that you are eating a few natural sugars such as those found in fruit and veggies. You don't want to have zero carbohydrates in your eating plan. Carbohydrates make you feel better. Just eat them without the added sugar, oil or fat.

- **A headache** – This could be the result of drinking less caffeine. But, should you find that you're getting severe headaches, do check your hydration. You may not be getting adequate water. If you were used to plenty of sugary drinks, it can be very hard to suddenly drink plain water. But, it's imperative that you drink enough water every day.

- **Anxiety** – Anxiety shows itself in many ways to diverse people. Some people get a jittery feeling in their stomach. Others experience heart palpitations or shortness of breath. It can be very extreme in some people. If you find that you're experiencing worry and anxiety, it is better to go to your doctor for a blood test. Illnesses like hypothyroid which have nothing to do with sugar restriction often cause anxiety. Otherwise, check your hydration level, sleep pattern, and make sure that you're eating adequate calories for your ideal weight.

- **Irritable Mood** – Feeling irritable? When blood sugar gets too low you feel moody. This can be relieved by eating more often. Attempt to balance your meals with the correct amounts of protein, fat, and carbohydrates for your personal requirements. Don't let yourself get too insatiable; this is a sure-fire way to end up feeling moody. Keep healthy snacks nearby such as apples, but no sugar or added peanut butter.

- **Fatigue** – Do you still feel that great big 3 p.m. slump? Feeling tired and foggy headed at the same time at work? This is a sure sign that you're not eating enough carbohydrates. Remember that veggies are also good carbs and you should eat them in good amounts. Or it can mean that you need to drink more water.

- **Achy Muscles** – This is one of the biggest signs of dehydration. Many people who are used to drinking sugary drinks for hydration often find it very difficult to get enough water. You need to drink at least eight glasses of water per day. For snacks, eat hydrating food such as apples, carrots, oranges and other fresh fruit and veggies.

- **Cravings** – Whenever you detect you're getting super-strong sugar cravings, look at your list of things to do during your sugar cravings. You can still eat sweet things, but instead of candy or processed food, choose something fresh such as a bowl of berries or sliced carrots or apples.

The symptoms of sugar withdrawal are harder for some people than it is for others. Be persevering with yourself, but be patient. If you give in and eat processed sugar, make sure you drink plenty of water, move around, and prepare for the next time with a good healthy snack. Remember to try the greens and vinegar.

CHAPTER 5

Recipe Ideas to Keep Your Sugar Cravings at Bay

The best way to avoid eating excess sugar is to be prepared. If you're prepared with what food to eat in advance, particularly when you have a craving; feeling tired, and when you're hungry, you'll do well in sticking to your goals.

Frozen Fruit Dessert

This is a simple recipe idea and you can use your own food processor, high-speed blender, magic bullet or a gadget like the Yonana Frozen Healthy Dessert Maker. All you need to do is freeze any fruit that you want to use, and feed it through the blender or the food processor. It's very simple and tastes delicious.

Top Tip: Use the ripest fruit for the sweetest flavor.

Snacks

The better snacks have a very good balance of protein and fat. These low-sugar snack recipes or ideas can help you if you miss sugar.

Apples and Peanut Butter – Leave out the bread and simply slice up an apple, and spread peanut butter (with sugar-free peanut butter). The best peanut butter only has one ingredient and that is peanuts. The fiber in the apple will enable the sugar to digest slowly. The fat and protein in the peanut butter keeps you full.

Fiber Rich Loaf – Most people like bread, but it has a huge sugar lift. But, try making your own fiber-rich bread that is low in sugar and very healthy for you.

No Sugar, Fiber Loaf

1 cup hulled, salt-free raw pumpkin seeds
1/2 cup hemp seeds
1/2 cup raw peeled almonds
1.5 cups rolled oats
2 tbsp. Chia seeds

3 tbsp. Psyllium husk powder
1 tsp fine grain sea salt
1 tbsp. Honey
3 tbsp. Apple sauce
1.5 cups water

- Combine all dry ingredients.
- Set aside.
- Combine all wet ingredients in a separate bowl.
- Then pour the wet ingredients into the dry.
- Mix until it forms thick dough.

If you notice that the texture is too dry, you can add more water. Form the mixture into dough and place it into a prepared bread pan. You can prepare the bread pan with some oil with a brush or paper towel, or you can line the pan with parchment paper.

Cover your pan and dough with a towel and let it sit in a warm place for at least two hours. When the dough has raised enough, you will know because it keeps its shape when you poke it gently with your finger.

Bake in a 350-degree F, oven on the middle oven rack for around 30 to 40 minutes. Baked bread will sound hollow when tapped.

Fermented Veggies

Chop up a bunch of veggies, or you can go to the grocery and buy pre-chopped veggies in bags, or from the salad bar. It's up to you how you do it. But, you'll want to chop them smaller anyway. Probably 1/2 inch pieces will work best.

In addition, you need some glass jars with sealable lids, such as canning jars.

Chop a mixture of veggies that you really enjoy eating. Include at least a couple of apples or carrots due to the sweet flavor they provide. Add some ginger if you like the flavor. Sprinkle it all with salt.

Fill each jar with the mixture of chopped veggies tightly. Leave one inch of space from the top. Push the veggies into the jar; you will want them very tightly packed. Then into each filled jar, put the following mixture into the jar until its one inch below the top.

Brine

4 cups water
1 tbsp. Sea salt

Mix until the salt is completely dissolved.

Ensure that your veggie mixture stays under the water in the jar. If you need to, weight the mixture down with a stone or weight. Cover with some cheesecloth and a rubber band. Keep in a warm spot for three to five days.

Check the mixture daily to ensure that everything stays under the brine. You'll know when your fermented veggies are done when your veggies are bubbling. That shows that the fermenting process has completed. Your veggies should smell a little sour, but you should like the smell. They should also taste really good. After which put the normal lids on the jars and place in the fridge.

CHAPTER 6

What Now?

If you really wish to rid yourself of sugar cravings, feel great, lose weight and become healthier, the best way to do it is to eliminate the added sugars. Remember, sugar is naturally in plants that you eat, which is okay, although you should try to limit super-sweet fruit such as dried fruits and dates.

Make sure you take it one day at a time and whenever you are hungry focus on eating until you feel full and satisfied but not stuffed up. Drink plenty of water, get enough daily exercise, and sunshine (when it shines), and you'll soon kick your bad sugar habit to the curb very soon.

Emotions

In this chapter, I am going to tell you about the role of emotions.

Our emotions can play a vital role in how and when we eat and this can be a vicious cycle in the world today. There is so much temptation and things that happen to make us feel depressed and down. The easiest thing in the world is to reach out to a sugary snack? So let us now discuss emotions a little more...

Lifestyle Choices: Learn to Overcome Emotional Overeating

Overcoming emotional overeating appears overwhelming, and setbacks are expected. But the good news is there are lifestyle choices that you can make to help overcome this problem.

The key word here is choice – so you can choose to follow a healthy lifestyle. Sometimes it helps to break things down into small, specific steps and milestones you can take and reach as trying to lead a "healthier lifestyle" seems a bit vague and airy fairy.

The following are some of these specifics, but remember, setbacks and relapses are normal. Don't beat yourself up; just start fresh tomorrow.

Exercise

Regular exercise three to five days a week is most beneficial according to experts. This exercise should consist of at least 20 minutes of cardiovascular exercise (vigorous walking, fast swimming, jogging, biking, etc.) followed by some light toning or weight training. Committing to this regimen full-force is not necessarily the best way to go; if you can only exercise once or twice a week, that's still better than nothing and will hopefully pave the way for more in the future.

Exercise is said to relieve emotional overeating in many ways. For one, exercise produces endorphins which are the body's natural "feel good" hormones.

For another, exercise stops boredom and mindless and endless eating, which is what you would be doing if you weren't exercising!

And finally, exercise will likely boost your self-image, helping to break the cycle of low or poor self-esteem and poor self-image that only "feeds" emotional overeating disorder.

Nature

Never underestimate the healing force of nature. For those with the emotional overeating disorder, choosing to pass more time out in nature can be exceedingly good. After all, in the natural realm there are no social media or picture messages to mess with your self-image or your head, and being in nature connects you to your origins and the origins of proper food.

Some experts theorize that detachment from food and its natural source can act a role in emotional overeating. Becoming involved in nature, exploring and appreciating it helps in reconnecting with our biologically normal view of food. Perhaps kill two birds with one stone and perform your regular exercise outdoors too.

CHAPTER 7

Alternative Therapies for Emotional Overeating

Emotional overeating can give the feeling of being imprisoned - it can appear as if there is no way out of this vicious cycle and make you feel angry, sad, and anxious; then you are eating to lessen the emotional pain. There are treatments available, but some of them more conventions and others an alternative.

Conventional therapy such as surgery, and medicine were used at one time or another for treating emotional overeating. Other alternative therapies are also worth you researching. Here are a few of them.

Hypnosis

Emotional overeating begins in the mind, hypnosis is meant to be effective only because it tackles the mind directly with suggestion.

Hypnosis is not the woo-woo stuff of swinging pocket watches; it's a scientific, clinical practice that practitioners have practiced with great success in treating emotional overeating.

Meditation

With meditation for emotional overeating you "tune in" to the emotional thought center, which drives your sugar cravings or binge eating. Meditation, a form of "mindfulness," is the direct opposite of mindlessness; often the result happens of emotional overeating. The person is not really thinking about what they are doing; this is mindless eating.

Herbal Supplements

Where ever you look, a new herbal supplement promises to help you lose weight. There are some herbs that can offer help with the issue of emotional overeating and here are some of them.

* Hoodia – A much-publicized herb that is supposed to suppress the appetite and boost energy levels. The effects are subtle, and it has a good safety record.

* Vitex - This hormone-balancing herb for women can assist those whose emotional overeating is swayed by hormone fluctuations.

* Ginseng - This very old, ancient herb apparently helps sugar cravings and curbs any compulsion to overeat in response to your ever changing emotions. American and Asian ginseng are claimed to be equally effective.

Acupuncture

Acupuncturists claim they can help with weight loss and in general, the result is yes however, not forever. The good news is that acupuncture is more successful with treating emotional overeating rather than overeating. This could be because acupuncture's alleged ability to release 'feel good' endorphins, and boosts metabolism, thus you feel

better emotionally, and this
effectively restraining emotional
overeating.

Nutrition

Having the right amount of vitamins
and minerals could affect emotional
overeating as nutritional deficiencies
could play a part in gluttony.
Therefore, make certain you don't
consume too much artificial, pre-
packaged, processed food; choose
fresh, whole foods as a general rule.
It's a good idea to take vitamin and
mineral supplements formulated for
your gender or life situation.

Weight Loss Surgery: Can It Help with Emotional Overeating?

Should you experience problems with emotional overeating, you could look into weight loss surgical operation. But do you know if it's really for you? What kinds of surgery options are available? Here are a few ideas to the general surgical options available at present, and some of the better-known advantages and disadvantages associated with them.

1. **Lap-Band**

A restrictive weight loss surgery, but it is adjustable. There is a silicon doughnut shape ring placed around the top of the stomach, allowing a small pouch above the ring; where the food goes at first, and this small pouch will fill up very quickly one feels full with less food. Gradually, the food makes its way from the pouch into the main stomach.

Occasionally the doctor or surgeon may inject saline into the ring to inflate it, decreasing the pouch's capacity even further if required. The opposite can be done too.

Pros:

* It's adjustable, as mentioned above – with fluid either removed or injected into the ring.
* The digestive process is not compromised; food can be digested in a normal way.
* Most times, the surgical procedure is done laparoscopically, meaning it's minimally intrusive.

Cons:

* You may need additional surgery in the case the access port twists or, perforation of the stomach occurs.
* Weight loss is slow but gradual, and not as dramatic other options.

* Repeated follow-up visits with your doctor are necessary.

2. **Gastric Bypass**

The malabsorptive technique. In gastric bypass surgery, a small pouch is created at the top of the stomach using "staples" unlike the donut ring. Part of the small intestine is re-routed so that it is connected to this pouch, creating a permanently smaller stomach. It is called "bypass" surgery because food bypasses the remaining stomach and the original small intestine connection, called the duodenum.

Pros:

* Weight loss seems to be greater and permanent.

* There are mild side effects, like heartburn, but this can be resolved easily.

Cons:

* Restricted nutrient absorption is a main concern; patients are normally required to take supplements to prevent nutritional deficiency.

* Dumping syndrome; fast emptying of the stomach contents, is a potentially problematic side effect.

* It's difficult for doctors to view the stomach and intestine via endoscopy, therefore cancer and other problems may go undetected.

These are just a few of the common types of weight loss surgery. So, weight loss surgery can offer help with the excessive weight gain and large caloric intake associated with emotional overeating; however, it will not address the underlying emotional problems. If you choose surgery, it's a good idea to make sure it's part of a holistic treatment plan that will include counseling and emotional therapy.

CHAPTER 8

Nutritional Treatments for Emotional Overeating

It may seem strange to refer to nutritional treatments for emotional overeating because the problem is too much eating? So why would you wish to look at more foods that you need to eat? Experts see more connections between nutrition and emotional overeating.

When you overeat in response to your emotions, you are not normally eating healthier foods. You become full or sick binge eating junk foods, therefore no good food is consumed. You do need the right nutrients to be healthy, and it then becomes a matter of quality verses quantity.

Nutritional Deficiencies

Another characteristic of emotional overeating may be nutritional deficiencies; deficiencies bring on cravings. The theory is that your body craves particular foods as a response to a need – such as in emotional overeating, this need is your feelings, but it may be physical as well. For example, a craving for sweet ice cream could signify your body's need for calcium.

See these examples of vitamins and minerals that, in accordance with research, are associated with the management of emotional overeating.

Vitamin D

This vitamin's effect on our mood is well-documented, and it's been suggested for people who have certain depressive disorders, such as SAD (Seasonal Affective Disorder). Foods that are high in Vitamin D include:

* Cod liver oil

* Sockeye salmon
* Soymilk (fortified with Vitamin D)
* Cow's milk

Remember Vitamin D is a fat-soluble vitamin, so sources with healthy fats, such as fish, could be absorbed far better by the body.

B-complex Vitamins

This group of important vitamins will help to increase energy levels and manage water retention. Foods with B vitamins include:

- Yogurt
- Eggs
- Lean beef (B12)
- Dark leafy greens (kale, broccoli, spinach)

Magnesium and Calcium

This is a powerful duo - many supplements place them together in one capsule or pill. These minerals are good for managing muscle and nerve tension. When these minerals occur naturally in foods, there is normally a higher proportion of magnesium to calcium, whereas supplements generally have more calcium than magnesium. Foods include:

* Beans
* Nuts, especially peanuts, hazelnuts, and pecans
* Corn

Zinc

Zinc has been shown to have a profound effect on appetite and cravings, and many people with eating disorders are deficient in this mineral. Zinc is found in the following foods:

- Shellfish, especially oysters and crab
- Beef, particularly beef shanks
- Pork
- Chicken
- Garbanzo beans

Deciding to make conscious choices on what you eat goes a long way when managing emotional overeating. Plan your meals in advance and make a shopping list; be proactive about meeting your nutritional needs.

CHAPTER 9

Emotional Bad Habits

The idea of whether state of minds comprises of bad habits is an intriguing one. Lots of mood disorders and conditions have been discovered and identified. These and other emotional problems are seen by some as purely bad habits.

As a matter of fact, it has been revealed that dwelling in your present bad mood only bolsters it. When you decide to act as if you are happy, research studies reveal that you could in fact enhance your mood in time. This is no set rule, yet there is some indicator that individuals do have some control over their moods.

Grumpiness, for example, could be more than bad habits for lots of. It might be bipolar disorder or other psychological issue. However, for some it might just be that they are giving in to every feeling that comes along. They have the bad habits of

not aiming to have any kind of
control over their whims.

Being pessimistic is just one of the
bad habits that can also be seen as a
sign of anxiety. Yet, for numerous, it
is just a habit of thought. They may
tell themselves that pessimism is a
win-win point of view.

If thngs go right, you win. If they go
wrong, you were right, so you win.
These people could enhance their
bad mood or grumpiness by
considering the positive side of
things initially.

Being in a distressing mood
resembles being downhearted. The
difference in between both bad
habits is that when you fret, you
become obsessed and fear any future
events. If you have the bad habit of
stressing, you could slowly train on
your own out of it, particularly if you
have the best type of help.

Codependency is not specifically a
mood, but it is a mood. It is a
collection of bad habits that
motivates a loved one to do unsafe

behavior. You do not desire your boy to be an alcoholic, as an example.

Nonetheless, you regularly make justifications for his habits to others. If you desire him to get much better, you have to stand and also decide to quit with your bad habits. You need to hold him liable for his actions.

If you have hypochondria, you have an emotionally painful bad habit. Definitely, a person with hypochondria needs mental aid. Nevertheless, the treatment that person will get will most likely focus on helping them transform their bad habits of thought. They will certainly discover new ways to think about illness and also their own bodies. This will certainly provide some control over their emotions.

If you do a lot of attention seeking, you have bad habits that you could learn how to abandon. This might relate back to something in your past. Possibly, you were neglected as a youngster because there were a few other needier people in the home. You found out bad habits of obtaining focus by irritating methods. Subjugating this bad habit calls for recognition of it, and possibly professional assistance.

Bad habits that associate with emotional states are frequently tough to break. Occasionally you require help to overcome them if you can refrain from doing it on your own. The faster you stop doing your emotional bad habits, the better your life will be.

CHAPTER 10

If Sugar is bad for you - are Sugar Substitutes Better?

SUCROSE is made from sugar beetroots or sugar cane. Not only does sucrose taste excellent, yet it likewise gives you quick power also. Nevertheless, the downside to this fast energy burst is that when it's gone, your body desires one more dose of sugar to keep the energy going. Absorbing way too much sucrose leads to extreme insulin responses, which causes the excess carbohydrates to be kept in your fat cells. Due to the fact that sucrose is a high-glycemic (rapid launch) sugar, you must substitute other sugar. Here are a few other types of sucrose to avoid when considering labels: raw sugar, brownish sugar, invert sugar, turbinado, confectioner's sugar, walking stick sugar, crystallized walking cane juice.

HIGH FRUCTOSE CORN SYRUP is made from corn starch and also has a high glycemic value which means it will trigger a huge insulin reaction. There is some conflict over the security of utilizing large quantities of this sugar with time. High fructose corn syrup is discovered in many items and is not the same as an item which contains fructose.

ASPARTAME has to do with 200xs sweeter compared to sugar and there is a great deal of problem over the security of this sweetener. It is made from 2 amino acids, aspartic acid and also phenylalanine. Aspartame is marketed under the names NutraSweet and equivalent and also is found in a wide range of ready products. This sweetener is not helpful for cooking or adding to hot beverages.

DEXTROSE OR GLUCOSE, has a greater glycemic worth than table sugar as well as on a lot of glycemic indexes, glucose is used to contrast the value of other "foods" as glucose (which is actual blood sugar) has a faster release right into your system than a lot of other sugar or food product which will certainly lead to a really sharp surge in your insulin degrees. Diabetics ought not to use this sweetener. On labels it could additionally be called corn sugar.

MALTITOL, like all sugar alcohols does not promote dental caries as well as having a taste and also sweetness like sugar. It does not increase blood sugar level levels or insulin levels and also works for diabetics. Like all sugar alcohols, maltitol could have a laxative result in some individuals.

SACCHARINE has been around for nearly 100 years as well as is 200xs sweeter than sugar. It is created from a compound discovered in grapes. The body cannot simplify, so it does not produce an insulin action. It is most typically discovered in sodas and also sugar like sweet and low.

HONEY, is an invert sugar formed by an enzyme from nectar. It is a combination of fructose, sucrose, glucose and maltose and also is a high glycemic sugar so it needs to be prevented by diabetics who have to control insulin. Unlike common belief's, honey only consists of trace amounts of minerals and vitamins.

Everybody recognizes that sugar is not a great component of a healthy and balanced diet, therefore many people are relying on sugar alternatives to get their craving for sweets satisfied, however, are these replacements actually much better compared to sugar or are there a lot more things concealed under the surface of these "much healthier" choices than fulfills the eye? Allow's take a better take a look at a few of these substitutes and see which ones are better and also which ones may be much better to prevent.

SUCRALOSE, sold under the name Splenda, serves as a one to one alternative to sugar. Sucralose is made from sugar and also is utilized to make Splenda, which tastes like sugar. Sucralose has no calories but does not determine, look or imitate sugar. Sucralose is 600xs sweeter compared to sugar so much less is needed for the same sweetness.

Sucralose is expanded with maltodextrin, a carbohydrate stemmed from corn, providing it some calories and also making it look and also act like sugar. This combination makes Splenda. Splenda has 1/8 to 1/4 the calories of sugar. We are told that all the sucralose taken in will be excreted unused, however, regardless of the makes cases, sucralose is taken in as well as metabolized by the body. The FDA's "last regulation" record claims that 11% to 27% of sucralose is absorbed in human beings as well as the Japanese food sanitation council claims as high as 40% is taken in.

SORBITOL is a sugar alcohol which is located in countless items, particularly those that should become completely dry or solidified sweet or confectionaries. Sorbitol is typically used in decreased calorie or light items.

LACTOSE, additionally called milk sugar is about half way between sucrose and fructose on the glycemic index. It is made from whey as well as skim milk and is used greatly by the pharmaceutical market.

As you could see, some sugars as well as alternatives could be fine to use instead of table sugar however definitely NOT every one of them. For diabetics or people attempting to control their insulin for weight loss, careful consideration must be taken when utilizing sugar or sweetened items. As for the remainder of us, well, still we need to be aware of exactly what kind of sweeteners we consume as you could not constantly rely on claims made by manufacturers of some sugar or products which consist of sugar regarding their safety or health and wellness benefits.

FRUCTOSE, additionally referred to as fruit sugar, is sweeter than table sugar as well as only 1/3 is required as a sugar replacement. Fructose is low on the glycemic index (slow launch sugar) and so it helps control insulin actions, maintaining them reduced, which suggests it is good for diabetics.

CHAPTER 11

Weight-loss vs. Weight loss - Yes There Is a Difference!

In order to slim down, your body must melt more calories than it takes in, however, keep in mind that your body requires calories for energy when you work out; your body needs even more calories. Before I speak about energy, the first point you should comprehend is that slimming down and losing fat is not the exact same point. Even if you lose weight, does not mean you lose fat, and even if you lose fat, does not mean you drop weight. When individuals discuss reducing weight, what the really want to do is lose the excess fat on their body as well as get an attractive number.

Keep in mind that the weight you had actually lost to begin with was mostly water weight and also you will ultimately gain it back in the form of fat, not muscule tissue (so as to get your muscular tissue mass back to the way it was in the past, you have to deal with restoring it). When carbohydrates as well as healthy protein that are currently in your body are used as the energy source, your body will certainly lose water weight since both carbohydrates as well as protein hold water in the cells. Essentially, you are dehydrating on your own to lose weight. So of course the scale will drop, yet roughly 75% (if not more) of it is water instead of fat. And also so you know, exercising while consuming a tiny calorie intake simply makes the circumstance worse. This is due to the fact that when you work out, you start burning off, more power and also the even more you exercise, the much more energy your body needs. I already informed you above where the energy originates from, and also if you do not provide your body the energy it requires, it will simply prey on your muscle mass also quicker since you are working out. So eat more food! In addition to this, when you cut down too much on your calorie consumption, your body will certainly start keeping calories since it doesn't know when you will certainly eat once again. The calories that are stored will be saved as fat. So simply puts, when your body is saving energy, it's primarily saving much more fat.

Make sure that you focus on weight loss not weight loss. Your objective should be to drop weight by melting fat, not losing water from your muscular tissues. Remember this when you select your weight reduction program.

When you consume, the body uses a lot of the calories for energy. If you consume much more calories compared to what the body makes use of, it will get to keep as fat. If you do not consume enough calories each day you will reduce weight, but you will certainly likewise lose power. When you do not eat sufficient power (calories) for your body, it will certainly begin consuming your power shops to make up for the energy deficiency. Unfortunately, the energy shops utilized is not your saved fat, however, rather, it's protein and carbohydrates (carbs) that will provide the majority of the power (saved fat comprises a really small percentage). Your body will certainly take the healthy protein and also carbs from your muscle mass cells; triggering your muscle mass to reduce (claim goodbye to that toned appealing look) which forces your metabolic process to reduce (a reduced metabolism = sluggish or lean burning). When this happens your body needs much less energy to preserve its new reduced body weight (remember the body weight is lower due to the fact that you loss, muscular tissue), which is why your body saves energy by reducing the metabolism. Putting it simply, the body has adjusted to the brand-new reduced power (calorie) intake which means that you will certainly no longer continuously lose weight.

Bottom Line: if you can't maintain that reduced calorie consumption for the rest of your life, you will certainly acquire your weight when you get tired of depriving on your own!

To summarize my point: Not consuming sufficient calories leads to muscle loss, dehydration, slower fat burning, as well as your body will certainly constantly adjust to a reduced calorie consumption.

To lose weight effectively (burning fat) you have to boost your metabolic rate (weightlifting) and also your demand for oxygen (aerobics) while eating sufficient calories every day (healthy diet plan) to offer you energy and preserve the healthy protein in your muscles due to the fact that healthy protein helps build muscle mass, which indirectly sheds fat. This brings up an additional good point: When you develop muscle mass your weight will boost since your muscular tissues are made up of mostly water, however, your body fat percentage will lower since developing muscle mass, increase your metabolic process (to put it simply, muscle mass way greater than fat, however use up much less space compared to fat). So keep in mind that shedding body fat can't be measured by a scale; utilize a gauging tape and take a look at yourself in the mirror, and then you will see real results. Among the very best methods to recognize if you are losing even more body fat compared to water is by using a body fat analyzer.

Weight-loss vs. Weight loss- Yes, Theres a Difference!

The Concern of Sugars - A Worthy Anxiety

There are individual who is considered to be morbidly obese if they are 100 pounds over their ideal body weight, and they have a BMI of 40 or more, or 35 or more and experiencing obesity-related health conditions, such as high blood pressure or diabetes. Therefore, it is important that the Bariatric person watch their sugar grams in food!

Concerning 97% of all Bariatric surgery clients learn to end up being very knowledgeable about what is referred to as the "unloading disorder", which is a method the body tells you that you ate something that you actually should not have consumed. "Dumping" turns up in several kinds from sudden tiredness, to nausea, to vomit, and even looseness of the bowels. When the "dumping" comes, remember of exactly what you most lately ate, and also do your best to prevent it again.

Many points can create unloading. Foods having too much grease, fats, carbohydrates, and sugars canister make you "dump." Yet the biggest wrongdoer in this list (yet numerous foods have these components in them), is sugar and sugar alcohols.

Just what are "Sugar Alcohols"?

Allow's say the food tag claims the item has 2 grams of sugar as well as 14 grams of sugar alcohols. Does that suggest it's safe? It is NOT safe due to the fact that when the sugar alcohols act similar to sugars, basically, you are taking in 16 grams of "sugar-action" since you have to add the two with each other given that they respond in the body similarly. Some "diet plan" foods claim to be low in sugar, true, but then, they consist of 22 grams of sugar alcohols. This is alright for non-bariatric patients, but a sure "discarding in the making" for us!

Sugar Alcohols might not add calories (as actual sugar does) to your body, but they do imitate sugar in the feeling they will make the

Bariatric client dump as if they engage of actual sugar. Usually, the Bariatric individual could not endure greater than 12 grams of sugar each dish. Beyond 12 grams of sugar will often cause some kind of disposing, be it moderate or severe. This is why it is essential to build up both the sugar and the sugar alcohols that are being consumed each dish.

Basically, Sugar Alcohols are artificial sweeteners or "anything that works as a sweetener in food but cannot be labeled as a sugar because it isn't really pure sugar."

Just what is "Sugar"?

Chemically, sugars are carbohydrates. As the body digests food, carbohydrates (other than fiber) damage down into sugars. We could locate sugars in a selection of types. Sugars just aren't made use of to sweeten food: they are likewise utilized as all-natural preservatives as well as thickeners. Sugars are included in foods throughout handling as well as prep work. The body cannot tell the difference between "natural" sugars as well as fabricated sugars due to the fact that they coincide in regards to chemical breakdowns.

"Incognito" Sugars

Keep an eye out for these sugars in disguise! Some are obvious while others are challenging:
- Maltose.
- Molasses.
- Fruit juice concentrates.
- Corn syrup
- Invert sugar.
- Table sugar (Sucrose).
- Raw sugar.
- Brown sugar
- High-fructose corn syrup.
- Honey.
- Fructose.
- Sugar (dextrose).
- Corn sugar
- Lactose.
- Syrup.

If you locate these things detailed on food tags, remember this: the item is most likely to be high in sugars if one of the above-mentioned shows first or second in the active ingredients list. If numerous of these are provided, then the item most-definitively will be too high in "sugars" for the Bariatric individual and also will certainly trigger unloading.

Also, fruits have "all-natural sugars". And also fruits, unlike packaged foods, do not have convenient wrappers on them, exposing any kind of sugar values within them. This is where we have to "recognize" what does it cost? Sugars are in the fruits we consume. Pineapple is among the highest natural-sugar fruits around, and also grapes are very high as well. Fruits benefit our system, if taken in moderation. Yet too much of the "natural" sugars could also create a bad result.

If you haven't created the anxiety of sugars by now, after that you could be doing yourself an injustice. It is necessary to recognize how sugars impact you directly so you could discover how to consume anywhere with confidence. When you start to understand just how sugars influence your system, you can after that attend any kind of gathering and understand exactly what is okay to consume and how much of that "event" food you could safely eat without causing an unpleasant and also inconvenient unloading episode. When you're discarding, attention is naturally attracted to you since others really care and will certainly ask about why you're not feeling well. If you don't want this type of focus, after that obtain your Sugar Intake Safety Area down to a personal scientific research for you so you could always loosen up and enjoy your food.

CHAPTER 12

Quiz Are You Addicted to Sugar? Is Healthy And Balanced Weight Difficult?

Research has revealed that foods containing high amounts of basic carbs, like sugar and also white flour, affect the chemical balance in your brain. These foods increase the level of serotonin, a natural chemical that makes you really feel calmer, extra certain, and a lot more relaxed.

When the sugar degree in your blood decreases once more, as it does quickly after a high-sugar snack, your serotonin levels likewise drop. This will certainly cause you to feel nervous, short-tempered and also stressed, so you grab one more snack. This backwards and forwards roller coaster in state of minds could bring about sugar dependency, without you also knowing it.

It's impossible to preserve a healthy weight management, diet if this cycle has actually become a full-blown sugar addiction.

To see if you're addicted to sugar, take the adhering to test:

- Do you discover potato chips, biscuits or snacks in your grocery store cart, despite the fact that you promised on your own you would not get any kind of snacks? Can you envision seeing your favorite television show or most likely to a flick without having a snack?

- Do you really feel "strange," or a little woozy, regarding the very same time every day? Do you "fix" your awkward symptoms with a journey to the sweet machine, or by grabbing a muffin at Starbucks?

- Do you really feel a little bit worried or protective if a person recommends that you may be consuming way too much sugar?

- Do you assume you could lower any time you wanted to, however, just haven't chosen it deserves it yet?

- Do you discover it challenging to stay on any type of nourishing, healthy and balanced diet because you begin consuming concerning a sweet bar or sandwich?

- Exactly what is your home cooking?

- When you feel down or depressed what type of foods interest you?

- Does stress and anxiety or clinical depression lead you to the breadbox or cookie container?

- How typically do you consume high-sugar foods, noodles, bread or pasta?

- Is it every day, or perhaps lot of times a day?

- Could you imagine a day without these foods?

- Do you occasionally really feel puffed up or obtain indigestion after eating specific foods, however still eat them anyway?

- Do you have any type of trouble sleeping, or get up around 3 am?

- Do you commonly feel lethargic, moody or depressed?

- If you addressed "yes" to two or even more of those questions, you've probably tried at least one diet in the past. Even if you take care of to lose some weight, you most likely get it back, due to the fact that you unconsciously long for sugar.

- A healthy and balanced diet is almost impossible to maintain until we get over the addiction, considering that sugar has lots of calories, yet nearly no nutrients. If you dominate your sugar dependency, you'll have a far better possibility of dropping weight as well as restoring your all-natural vitality.

Get Rid of Those Extra Pounds

If you do decide you want to lose weight (whether it be a few pounds or excess body mass), you've already done the research on diets, plans, gyms, exercises. If so, you've seen that most of the credible sources will inform you that losing weight and fitness are strongly related. If not, that's what I'll be telling you right now.

If you wish to lose weight, initially you need to consider a few home truths. The obvious one is that if you burn off more calories than you eat, you will lose weight. So you can chose either to do no "added" exercise and eat less in order to lose weight, or stick to a plan that will burn off enough calories and also allow you not to starve. Note that decreasing your calorie intake can backfire on you, because your body will slow your metabolism down in order to accommodate the adjustment in calorie intake. This will cause weight gain instead of weight loss..

The second fact is that a combination of water and oxygen leads to fat burning. Ensure you are getting at least a half-gallon of water each day. Your body uses the water when you exercise, and this enables you to lose weight in a healthy way. Again, you need to combine your water intake with a form of aerobic exercise (increased oxygen) for this to work. Choose something that you prefer and can continue with on a regular basis like walking, biking, rowing, swimming, yard work and so on. You must get your heart rate up a little bit, it's a good fat burning exercise.

Lastly, consistency is key with your weight loss and fitness plan. People jump into this quickly with the wrong mindset, they keep up for a few weeks or months and then they can go back to their usual unhealthy lifestyle.

To be successful at this your plan must be a life long commitment. Even after you lose the weight, you need to maintain your goal weight, and you need to eat right and be physically active. Therefore, choose an activity that you really enjoy. Walking is a favorite of mine and if you live in the city, walk part of the way to work; save on gym fees, and do not worry about finding time in the day to exercise. If not, no matter where you are, find time to take a 20-minute brisk walk around the block. Have a buddy to keep you entertained or listen to music and you'll see that the time flies. The connection between weight loss and fitness is far too strong to disregard. So, pick your plan and stick with it for the rest of your life.

Winter Weight Gain

That winter weight gain, especially after Christmas is quite normal, and it is perfectly acceptable to gain those extra pounds in the colder months, but remember too much weight can take longer to work off when the warm weather finally arrives. Winter is challenging when it comes to maintaining, or losing, weight. The days are shorter, the nights longer and all you want to do sometimes is to sit in a relaxing, comfortable chair beside the fireplace and snooze. But being mindful of a few tips, you may be able to avoid what is inevitable.

When it comes down to it, we are limited on outdoor activities in extreme winter climates. Indoor exercise can be boring to many people so it becomes a chore in comparison to outdoor exercising which makes you feel fitter. There is not much you can do to change this fact of moving your routine inside.

What you could do is make it short.
In fact, you could cut down your
work in half by varying its intensity.
Switch back and forth between
smaller bursts of high aerobic
exercise that gets you puffing and
rest periods where you simple calm it
down.

Pay attention to what you eat during
this winter period. Not what you eat
every day, but how it is presented;
how looks, smells and tastes in your
mouth. If you enjoy your meals and
snacks rather than just eating fast,
you can feel fuller and more satisfied.
The same goes along with trying to
stick to a healthy diet pattern. A good
rule is to eat about three moderate
meals and two healthy snacks per
day. Stick with fruit, vegetables, lean
meat, whole grain and fiber-rich
foods. Only eat nuts and cheese for
snacks rather than sweets or
processed foods.

Identify any patterns. If you've gained weight in the winter most times, try to understand why? Should you know why, do something about it to change the pattern. Most people eat out of boredom so try out a new exercise or hobby, perhaps take up a class in something.

Long holiday periods occur during the winter and often the biggest offender of all when it comes to winter weight gain. If you're cooking up heartwarming meals for the holidays, ensure you keep raw vegetables close hand to snack on and serve up healthy food alternatives too. If you're a guest at numerous parties, try to go for the healthier choice.

Buddying up with someone or joining a support group can help. It's easier to stick to your goals when you're held responsible by someone else who is also going for the same goals too.

Lastly, remember that winter weight gain is normal. While you don't want to be gaining pounds, don't get upset over a couple of extra ones. These can be easily lost as quickly as they were gained.

Zero Calorie Foods

Looking for a free list of zero calorie foods? These are the foods that actually burn more energy to consume than the calories they contain, so if anyone who wants to lose weight should go for these types of foods.

Here is a free list of zero calorie foods - some may surprise you:

- Celery
- Grapefruit
- Watermelon
- Lettuce
- Cauliflower
- Oranges
- Apples
- Strawberries
- Tomatoes
- Cucumbers
- Apricots
- Zucchini
- Tangerines
- Carrots
- Hot Chili Peppers

The great thing about zero calorie foods such as those in the above list is that they actually use up calories from other sources in your body, in order to be digested. So, eating such great calorie burners should definitely be included in any weight loss plan.

Remember that when your body runs short of energy from carbohydrate sources, the next place it looks for energy is in your fat! This is a wonderful way to get rid of excess fat in your body, and this is how zero or negative calorie types of foods to help you lose weight, feel great and maintain the weight that you achieve.

In general, zero calorie foods come from fruits and vegetables as shown in the list above. Other examples are pineapple, papaya, peach, honeydew and cantaloupe. These are valuable because of their zero calories and because they hold strong detox properties. Other vegetables include broccoli, green beans, asparagus and carrots. Celery is especially worthy because only holds 10% of the amount of calories required to digest this vegetable; the remaining 90% comes from elsewhere, like your fat stores.

Get the best results from these types of foods, alternate eating these with other healthy proteins, carbohydrates, whole wheat products and things that contain plenty of fiber. While you might enjoy eating such foods for a time, you can also tire of them, so don't get carried away. Choose one or two a days to substitute another meal or snack. A diet restricted to only these foods could lead to malnutrition. However, when it comes to snack times, these selections are real winners.

Also remember that losing weight isn't only about what you do and don't eat. Regular activity is key to shedding pounds. This part frightens many people because they imagine themselves having to go to an expensive gym or to go running for as long as an hour each day. The answer to the latter is – no, no at all.

Regular activity should be something you do to maintain your weight throughout your life, so you should look forward to doing (or, don't dread doing it). Regular exercise doesn't mean "every day" either. It really means "consistent". The best and easiest type of regular exercise is walking. Taking a 20 to 30 minute walk at least three to four times every week is considered regular activity.

Linking the free list of negative calorie foods with a healthy, well-balanced diet and steady activity will get you where you would like to be with your weight goal.

Water Retention

If water retention is a major problem for you, then you probably want to find how much actual water weight you can lose to achieve the shape and weight you set as your goal. The solution to losing water weight is an odd one. If you are trying to lose fat, you are meant to eat less fatty foods. So it seems logical that to lose water weight you need to drink less water. This is far from the truth. The best way to lose water weight is to drink even more water. Let us look at why that is the case.

Why Do I Retain Water Weight?

The body requires water to be healthy. The body's most important functions depend on water to work efficiently. If your body detects that it isn't getting enough water to operate correctly, it assumes there is a drought going on and it will begin to conserve water! Your body releases a hormone that stops the kidneys from filtering it. Similar to when we are going through dry weather spells, with the water supply we then cut back on some of the excess usage and try to make do with as little water being used as possible. This can lead to a lot of other problems.

Can Drinking Water Cause Problems?

When you are not drinking enough water dehydration occurs, and this often leads to other serious problems. One major factor is that water helps eliminate both solid and liquid waste from the body. The water assists in moving things like toxins and fat along and out of your system. It also helps break down solid matter that your body has broken down and helps it transport easier. If it's not getting water, fecal matter remains in your system and brings about many other health issues. Lack of water also slows down your metabolism. It can keep any nutrients from flowing through your body like it is supposed to do so.

How Much Water Do I Need To Drink?

When you realize you aren't getting enough water, there is a tendency to overload on it. This won't help. Imagine when the rain comes after a long dry spell, and the ground is rock solid? The ground may absorb some of the rain water, but it has to have more moisture in it so as to absorb more water, like a sponge. All the excess water that it can't absorb runs off elsewhere. Inside your body, if it hasn't had enough water, it will not handle large quantities, and will simply transport it into the bladder. That is why you urinate so much when you drink a lot more water than you would normally.

A healthy amount for you to drink is between one half and two thirds of your body weight in ounces. If you weigh 200 pounds, then you should be drinking between 100-133 ounces of water per day. This takes getting used to, so when your body is getting used to drinking water, it will start to believe that the drought is over and so there is less of a need to retain as much water.

How much water weight you lose is subject to how much water you drink (making sure you get enough), how much exercise you do, and how healthy you eat.

Eating Regularly

It is awesome how much weight can be lost by eating more food. Many people believe that to lose weight you need to be eating less. But less, usually means, less often. This isn't essentially the case, though.

You may already know that the most important meals of the day is breakfast. It is shame seem to have less time for it during a busy week. We get caught up in going to work that we end up abandoning the one meal that may end up making the rest of the day seem better. We get a hungry and have our morning fix by having our favorite snack bar or a large muffin or Danish pastry of some kind. This is not the best thing for us to eat. We might curb our hunger pangs a little while, but our bodies will be deprived of any good stuff later on.

What are the benefits of eating breakfast?

1) It's just like filling up your car gas tank first thing in the morning. Having a healthy breakfast helps you get more done through the day without being interrupted. It won't mean that you won't feel hungry, but you will start the day off with the best kind of energy and your blood sugar levels will be at a balanced level at that. This means you will feel better with less down time.

2) Your brain and nervous system will function properly. It essentially enables your synapses to fire on all cylinders. Your brain is much sharper and focused plus your decision making skills are far better. Your memory improved too.

3) Breakfast makes us far less prone to binge eating. If you need to wait until lunchtime to eat on an empty

stomach, you will feel hungrier. Of course, this means that you will try to find more food to eat and will make you less selective in your choice. You want to stop the hunger so you go to the closest sandwich bar or fast food chain and buy the biggest burger you are secretly carving. Not only will you too much, you will eat it very fast. Eating fast means you are eating far more than you really need. You are getting food down you so fast from being hungry that your body doesn't really have the time to figure out when it's full, until it's too late.

4) Eating breakfast does help you lose weight so don't skip it. It's not only breakfast, though. It's eating regularly, several times a day. Eat early and often to lose the most weight. Breakfast plays a very important role in the grand scheme of things. If you skip meals, your body starts to think that it's starving and will go into storage mode thinking there is a famine on and it must self preserve as much as

possible. That is when it all turns into blubber, fat. It can slow down your entire metabolism and your ability to actually burn the fat. When you eat that healthy breakfast, you are letting your body know that you won't be starving for the rest of the day, so it doesn't have to panic about storing it. It also gets your metabolism working and ready to burn fat all day.

When you have breakfast and regular meals throughout the day, you will really be surprised with how much weight can be lost if only you decide to eat more, healthy food of course...

Natural Weight loss

Natural weight loss with herbs can occur if you know which herbs work and are safe for you. They can become a safe alternative if you research and educate yourself on how they actually work and how they interact with your body. Not all herbal weight loss products are safe for you. While many will safely help your body lose excess weight, there are others which could be extremely harmful for you, even though they may be safe for some other people.

Here are some herbs that are considered to be safe and effective in weight loss when used correctly.

-Alfalfa works as a diuretic and has components that help make fat more soluble and helps your blood vessels stay healthier.

- Chickweed assists in the breakdown of fat molecules. Used with burdock root which will help remove the fat molecules and purify the blood.

- Cayenne pepper has capsaicin and it helps with blood circulation and digestion. It works by increasing your core body temperature influencing your body's metabolism, helping it to rise. This too helps with weight loss.

- Dandelion Root works in the liver by helping to clean the body of it's toxins making your body metabolize fat a lot better.

- Fennel Seed apparently increases your energy level, and assists to reduce hunger pangs. Used with nettle in tea to help with weight loss.

*Beware and not go over the recommended amount of fennel seed because in large doses it can be toxic.

Check with a professional / your doctor to find out how much fennel is a healthy portion to ingest.

-Flax Seed is a wonderful source of protein and fiber. It has many phytonutrients and vitamins and is one of the best aids in obtaining a healthier body. It helps curb your appetite if it is taken about 20-30 minutes prior to meals. It is a bulk laxative so, expect results.

-Green Tea is a popular product that helps your metabolism to burn fat as it raises energy, similar to caffeine in giving you more energy.

-Hawthorn Berry helps remove food that has trouble breaking down in your stomach, assists the adrenal glands by stimulating them, and improves the thyroid gland.

*Check with your doctor when using this because if you have a thyroid condition or you are taking medication for your thyroid, hawthorn could have an adverse effect.

There are many other herbs that people had success with for weight loss. Before trying any of these, talk to your doctor and/or an herbalist and find out how it may affect you and respond with medications or other supplements you are taking. It is enticing to find everything in pill form. While this might be convenient, a better method in achieving natural weight loss with herbs is to seek fresh or whole dried herbs and use them as much as possible.

Should you be looking for a "magic pill" that will bring about weight loss you may have looked into herbal weight loss pills that claim to be a "safe and natural" way to lose weight. Are those ways safe?

For some people, there is an involuntary assumption that just because something is natural that it is safe. Well, snake venom occurs naturally, but I wouldn't ingest it. Peanuts are natural and good for most people, but for others it can bring about a severe allergic reaction that needs quick medical attention. Just because something is "natural" doesn't mean that it is that safe. Even if it is safe for some people, doesn't mean that it is safe for you. So always check with a professional.

What does this have to do with herbal weight loss?

Herbal products used for weight loss practice a variety of ways which are meant to help you in losing weight. Most of these weight loss products that are considered herbal will either trick the brain into thinking it is full.

Many more will use thermogenics to help speed up their metabolism.

What are some of the herbs used for weight loss that need to be avoided?

First, avoid anything that is an herbal laxative. Buck-thorn, cascara, rhubarb root, and Senna are a few of the ones you will see most often on the market. The danger in using laxatives to lose weight is because it can bring about dehydration, constant cramping and basically, diarrhea. The muscles used to control bowel movements can become weakened to the point whereby you cannot control them. You can also become addicted to taking such laxatives and you can risk becoming bulimic.

Ephedra, also known as ma-huang, is probably the perilous ingredient to look out for the most. There is a related product known as herbal phen-phen (or fen-fen) that has ephedra as the main ingredient; known to raise the blood pressure and increase your heart rate. It can also really mess up your central nervous system, causing over stimulation. Some of the side-effects of ephedra or ma huang are seizures, stroke, heart palpitations, or heart attack. There are deaths that have been associated with the use of ephedra.

What herbal products are there that are safe and can help in effective weight loss?

Three main ones are:

Cayenne, green tea, and seaweed.

As I mentioned earlier, cayenne has capsaicin which safely helps stimulate digestion and increases your metabolism.

Green tea is a safe stimulant that gives you a healthy amount of vitamin C.

Seaweed stimulates the thyroid which can help in weight loss. But make sure that you check with your doctor if you have thyroid problems or are on thyroid medications before using it.

There are many other herbal weight loss products that are safe, but there are also many others which aren't. Just like the peanut, there may be some that are healthy for some people, but are hazardous to others. No matter which one you use, check with your doctor first to make sure that it is safe for you.

Garcinia Cambogia an extract, derived from a tropical fruit found in Africa and India, is a natural weight loss supplement which is becoming increasingly popular in the West. A relatively new discovery in the industry so not enough studies have been conducted in order to verify solid conclusions, but some people claim that they benefited from this extract.

Garcinia Cambogia a member of the citrus family is inedible because of its extreme sourness, but the rind of this fruit is often used when cooking dishes in India. Hydroxycitric acid (HCA) is now being extracted from the fruit and it is processed in the form of a weight-loss supplement.

One of the advantages of hydroxycitric acid is that it doesn't have that "fluttery or jittery effect" on the brain like caffeine in coffee do. Also, it does not suppress your appetite like many other supplements. The problem with weight loss aids that trick the brain is that, when you stop taking them, you will again start to crave food. Instead, HCA works because it provides your body with extra energy, causing the body to tell the brain that is not hungry.

Keep in mind is that Garcinia Cambogia extract of works best when it is combined with chromium (used to regulate the blood sugar level), especially because many people in the US are not getting enough chromium. Chromium deficiency could be one possible reason for obesity and diabetes.

Who are the best candidates for hydroxycitric acid, HCA?

HCA works remarkably well for those who eat when they are anxious, depressed, upset, sad, etc. (pertains to many individuals). This is because HCA has the same "filling" effect on such people, as food does.

Another advantage of taking hydroxycitric acid is that you do not need to follow any "special diet" as you ingest it. Although you need to eat balanced, healthy meals and snacks; your weight loss should be slow but steady. Try to eat smaller amounts of food, but don't skip meals or starve yourself. Replace sugary snacks or fried food, with fruit, vegetable, cheese and/or nuts. It's a good idea to try to exercise too. There is no need to go to extremes, but be consistent with activity, this is key to healthy weight loss.

There are a few studies conducted on HCA. In fact, more research has been done on this than any other weight loss product. HCA does not have any side effects and you can buy it online.

A few words of warning include:

If you have diabetes, you should consult your doctor before taking any chromium. If you are pregnant or breastfeeding, consult your doctor before taking HCA. Caution should be exercised when it comes to obese children. Lastly, citrus fruits can upset and aggravate arthritis and migraine sufferers, so if you suffer

from either, avoid taking Garcinia
Cambogia extract completely.

Low Carb Diet

Low carbohydrate dieting appeals to a large number of people, mainly because of the claim to quick results. However, prior to opting in to this kind of plan, you need to make sure that you understand everything involved.

A low carb diet mainly focuses on eating plenty of protein and limiting (or eliminating altogether) carbohydrates. The reason for limiting carbohydrates is that they are quickly and easily converted into and stored as fat. In theory, by eating few or no carbohydrates, you limit the possibility of anything being turned into fat. Then, this is meant to cause you to lose fat (weight). But the question is. Does low carb dieting truly work?

As with many "quick fix" weight loss

Diets, it does. But only for a limited time. What it comes down to is that your body requires carbohydrates. When it becomes starved of them, your body starts taking its energy from glycogen stores. Now for the science bit. . . For every gram of glycogen, there are four grams of water attached. So, what you are losing water when you lose weight; it is the water you lose. It appears to look like its working for a while, but as soon as you start eating carbohydrates again eventually you have to do), you will gain back all the water weight.

Keep in mind that any type of diet, which claims that you have to do it for a short while and then return back to "normal" eating habits, will not work. Instead of focusing on a diet, simply change your lifestyle and daily eating habits. This alarms many people because they think it means never eating a piece of chocolate or cake again. That is not true at all. In fact, it is the strict quick diets that are applying this kind of "no exception" concept. Then, when the diet ends (because you cannot continue to such strict restrictions), you will gain all the weight back!

An appropriate weight loss and maintenance program is doable over a long time. This requires placing healthy food into your body (healthy proteins, whole grains, fruits, vegetables, and fiber and Omega-3 fatty acids), and cutting down on the wrong things like sugar, processed and fried foods, etc.

Can you eat the bad ones every once in a while too?

Yes of course. But be mindful of how often you are doing it. Tto get the best results with losing weight and maintaining your goals, you need to be doing light, regular activity. Make it something that you enjoy or that fits into your daily schedule. Like walk to work (weather permitting). It might actually take the same amount of time as sitting in traffic in the car or on public transportation.

Low carb dieting is one of the various diets offering very short-term results. Stick to something more realistic that you can follow for a lifetime and keep the weight off for good.

CHAPTER 13

Menstrual Cycle

I thought I would touch on this subject because it is often when "that time of the month" is coming around that you start dreading many things. The most common problem is wondering how much weight gain is going to take place this time? Feeling bloated in the stomach. While it may feel like a balloon and appear to pile on the pounds, it is not as much as you imagine.

Of course, there is a level of discomfort that accompanies a bloating feeling, but it doesn't mean to say that you are putting on ten or twenty pounds during it. It feels like it, but you really, really aren't believing me. The truth is that there is only a difference of about 2-4 pounds, that is all.

So where does this damn weight gain come from?

There are many misunderstandings about where this weight gain comes from before menstruation. Many believe that it comes from overeating. After all, you do eat more during PMS, especially with chocolate, yes admit it. The truth behind the matter is that while there are more tears, tantrums and emotional eating going on in general, there is also an increase in metabolism that's enough to offset the difference. Okay, there may be just a mild increase, but not enough to be that noticeable despite you feeling it.

Another misconception is because of from eating more sweets perhaps. The fact is you are craving more and more sugar during pre-menstruation. It's not clear why this is the case, but it exists and the craving intensifies as the many symptoms of premenstrual syndrome worsen. Maybe to give a high before the onset of the other wretched symptoms, who knows.

While you might think that this would cause excessive weight gain each month, you aren't really eating, increased calories to cause very much of a surge in weight.

The weight that you do put on mainly comes from water retention. For those who are struggling to control their weight, this can be frustrating. It appears that despite how much work you do or how well you diet, you still seem to put on the weight and feel majorly bloated. Don't fret, though. The water that is reserved usually all comes off during menstruation.

There are, however, a few things that you can do to help limit the amount of water you retain.

1) Limit the amount of sodium you take in.

2) Increase the water you drink.

When you get more sodium (salt) than you require, it tends to stay in the intestines and needs more from the kidneys to flush it all out. Your body starts to need more water and if your body isn't getting water, it starts retaining it. It notices that it needs more and realizes it isn't going to get enough. When your body feels like it isn't getting the water it requires to function properly, it starts to go into conservation mode, remember. It starts using less and keeping more in reserve.

When you cut down the amount of salt and sodium you normally eat or drink, your body requires less water to function efficiently. When you know that your body is going to be retaining more fluids anyway because you are approaching your menstrual period, cut down on salt, and start increasing the amount of water you drink. In doing so, your body will want to retain less water and you won't need to wonder each

month how much weight gain is
going to take occur.

Pregnancy

For those fortunate enough to be pregnant, it's normal to want to find out how much weight should you gain during pregnancy. The answer is usually standard with everyone, although everyone will carry weight differently. Most of the time, you have been with the idea that excess weight gain is not good, but when you are pregnant, weight gain is a very good thing because it is a sign of a healthy baby. For the best answer to the question, ask your health care professional, but this book will give you an idea of what to expect.

The answer will vary from person to person based on their body size prior to pregnancy. Those who are underweight should gain more than those who are overweight. Underweight women should expect to gain anywhere from 28-40 pounds. The average weight person should gain 25-35 pounds, and the overweight woman should gain roughly around 15-25 pounds.

You should plan on gaining only about three or four pounds in the first trimester and then around a pound per week of the pregnancy. This, of course, will be more for those carrying more than one baby.

Here is a breakdown of how that extra weight is distributed.

- Approx 8 pounds of this will be the baby, eventually. This will vary for each child, but the average weight will be around 8 pounds.

- About 2-3 pounds of this will be placenta.

- Another 2-3 pounds will be amniotic fluid.

- 2-3 pounds for the extra breast tissue.

- 4 pounds of this is the extra blood supply.

- Anywhere between 5 -9 pounds will be in extra fat for the delivery of the baby, and for breastfeeding.

- The last 2-5 pounds will be due to an increase in the size of the uterus.

Should you feel you are gaining more weight, discuss it with your health care professional. Most likely you will not be gaining too much weight, but if you do, you should not try to lose weight. If you do lose weight, it could have a negative effect on the development of your baby. You should be keeping your health care professional informed about all changes going on so they can make sure that the baby is healthy.

If you are concerned about not gaining excess weight, try to eat more often during the day. Keep quick and ready t eat snacks at hand so that you can resolve those hunger pangs that come from nowhere. You are meant to be eating around 100-300 more calories per day when you are pregnant so eating foods that are high in protein and that will put you at the amount of calories you are supposed to be eating daily. Eat the extra goodness when you can, for your baby.

Whatever you do during your pregnancy, remember to keep your health care professional informed of what is happening. Voice any concerns and ask for their advice. They are the ultimate authority on questions like how much weight you should gain during pregnancy.

Brand new mothers from around the world often try to find how to lose stomach fat after C-Section. Despite the blessing of pregnancy and the birth, your body has undergone enormous pressure and stress. What you may have, especially after a C-Section, is a type of "apron" of fat hanging downwards. You have to cope and get used to dealing so much else and now that extra flab is around your belly, but it is one concern you should not need to worry too much about.

All new mothers have undergone this at some point, whether they had a C-Section or not. Many found ways to lose the extra. Not only does it appear unattractive, it can bring discomfort or pain. Here are some ways you could overcome this.

1- Pilates Exercises

Pilates is known to be a very safe and comfortable way of exercising that helps tone muscles and enables flexibility in your body so as to not stress it. It can be done safely by different people of all ages and physical conditions. This will help to get your body back in shape. Not only can it help your body, it is therapeutically similar to yoga. Your body was pressured. Pilates will eliminate stress and help bring peace back to it.

2- Walking

You may not be able to go out for a walk every day by yourself, but it is a great reason to show off your baby in the new stroller perhaps. Getting out in the fresh air and vitamin D from the sun is very good for both of you.

Try not to do too much too soon though. Do what feels comfortable. Walking is a great aerobic exercise and burns the fat everywhere. The extra weight will go. If you have a treadmill at home, try it out when your babies are having a nap. Don't work out at every nap time, though. You also need your rest, too.

3- Crunches & Flutter Kicks

Try to do certain exercises that focus on your abs. It will help tone the muscles underneath and this in turn burns fat. Crunches are fairly easy to do, but don't pressure yourself too much. Take it easy at first, find the correct way to do them safely. Flutter kicks are exercises that you can do lying on your back. Place your hands under the small of your back, and lift your legs a few inches from the ground. Simply make quick, but gentle, kicking motions similar to swimming on your back. Do this for a couple minutes a day and you will soon discover your ab muscles getting stronger and stronger. But again, don't push yourself too hard. If you feel any form of discomfort, stop what you are doing immediately.

Try to do these exercises and eat a well-balanced diet as it provides you with the food you need in order to recover; the right nutrition for your child too, especially if you are breast feeding, you will have found a great way how to lose stomach fat after a C-Section.

Problem Areas

One of the main problem areas that women experience is trying to find out how to lose weight from their thighs. This area seems to take forever, it seems. Many often give up the fight to get eliminate fat in their thighs, but don't let yourself be one in that group. There are many ways that you can effectively lose weight in your thighs.

Firstly, focus on is burning the fat. You cannot burn fat only on your thighs. You need to work on burning fat from everywhere. This can be done using aerobic exercise or activity. If you get your heart pumping and air moving around your lungs, fat will start melting away. At some point you will see the results in your thighs. But very the exercise and don't only do one aerobic activity. Do several and mix them up regularly.

The second thing you will need to do is check and monitor your diet. What you eat is going to influence the level of fat that you burn. Should you eat a lot of protein, then you are going to be providing your body with something that will give you more muscle. Don't cut back too fast on the amount of food you eat. Don't cut down on the amount you eat per day. If you eat more often during the day, your body decides it doesn't require as much fat to store, because it thinks that you aren't going to starve it. Clever isn't it?

Thirdly, you need to do is drink plenty of water. When you workout doing aerobic activity, the fat is going to begin dissolving. It has to work its way out of your system. Drinking plenty of water enables this to happen. Not only does it push fat and toxins out from your body, it will let your body know that there isn't any drought going on. Remember, when your body is deprived of water, it thinks it needs to retain water, and it starts to conserve it, using only a small amount of water to perform your body's basic functions. If you drink more water, you will lose more water. This means that you will also be losing some of the water weight around those problem thighs too.

The fourth thing you need to do is to focus on building muscles in your buttocks and thighs. The best exercise for this is doing squats. As you build muscle here, you will have more than toning occurring. If you increase your muscle mass, you then increase your metabolism. Likewise, if you increase your metabolism, you will increase your body's capability to burn fat.

So you need to remember to burn fat and to move more,; eat well and eat often, drink plenty of water, and build up your muscle. It might take a while to see the results, but if you do stick with it, you will definitely have the shape you desire for yourself.

CHAPTER 14

Goals

Make the commitment to lose weight and get in shape. Are you trying to decide how much weight you should try to lose? Setting realistic goals are most important. Setting the appropriate goals for you could be one of the hardest things to do. But not making goals can invite failure to your weight loss objective. What weight loss goals should you set for yourself? In order to set the best goals you need to know where you are at, set a long-term realistic goal, and give yourself rewards for meeting them.

Where You Are Now

It isn't only a matter of how much you may weigh, it is more a matter of noting an accurate assessment of where you are right now. Go visit your doctor to make sure that you are healthy enough to take on the challenge. Many people get started with a weight loss program only to find out that they can't complete it because their body can't handle the pressure or strain. Find out your true weight and get your body mass index (BMI) number. Get your measurements like your hip-to-waist ratio and your body fat percentage. It isn't necessary to have all of these, but it will help you to know from where you started, how you progress forward, and where you end up.

Decide Where You Want To Go

Make sure that you set realistic goals set for yourself. Going from a size 40 inch waist to a 30 inch waist may not be realistic for you. Going from a 40 inch waist to a 35 inch waist is fairly reasonable, but still ambitious. Losing 20 pounds is a realistic long-term goal. Losing 20 pounds in only two weeks really isn't a realistic one. Try to do aim for a goal that is realistic. Ensure you have a planned date for you to achieve that goal that is realistic as well. Don't try to do the impossible. Try to do what you are capable of doing. When you reach that goal, set a more ambitious one for yourself. Plan on setting for yourself short-term goals along the way to break it up a little.

Reward yourself and plan on doing something nice for yourself for reaching your long-term goal. Make it something special. Keep on telling yourself as often as possible. Don't just have one reward for yourself, though. For each little milestone you reach along the way, treat yourself to something special. Give yourself small prizes for being such a hard worker. This makes the long-term goal easier to reach.

If you are really serious about losing weight, give yourself a chance being realistic about your goals. Don't forget to reward yourself for the hard work you do. Figuring out how much weight should you lose is a good goal, but don't let that be the only goal you have.

Frequently Asked Questions

Is craving sugar a sign of diabetes?

No, craving sugar is not normally one of the symptoms of diabetes, or hyperglycemia the latter is too much blood glucose. Symptoms of diabetes are usually frequent urination, excessive thirst, fatigue, weight loss, and blurry vision. However, if you skip meals often you may be experiencing hypoglycemia, or low blood sugar.

What can cause you to crave sugar?

Eating added can cause sugar cravings to rise, leaving you feeling more tired and irritable. As your hormone levels start to change, your body will attempt to increase levels of the feel-good hormone serotonin, and as sugar activates a serotonin release, this can cause you to crave sugary things.

How do I get rid of my sugar addiction?

- Substitute whole fruit for sweets
- Eliminate artificial sweeteners if you can
- Have a backup plan
- Manage your magnesium levels

Can I lose weight by cutting out sugar?

Reducing your calories will only slow down your metabolism and make you feel hungry and weight loss will fail. Therefore eating a higher fat, higher protein, lower sugar and refined carb diet can speed up your metabolism and reduce your hunger.

How can I cut down on sugar or cut it from my diet?

- Stop eating processed foods for example, try making your own spaghetti/tomato Sauce
- Choose whole, fresh fruit over juice, dehydrated, or other fruit products
- Avoid eating flavoured yogurt
- Make your own salad dressing
- Give yourself a daily quota
- Have rules about dessert
- Avoid keeping treats in the house!

What vitamin deficiency causes sugar cravings?

Any deficiency is caused by the Crave Cycle so when you eat sweet things the sugar is ingested into your body and the sugar, then blocks the absorption of any essential minerals particularly calcium and magnesium. Scientific studies have proven that a deficiency in these two micro-nutrients causes the sugar craving.

Foods to stop sugar cravings

- When I'm craving a dessert, try sprinkling trail mix on plain yogurt to creamy, sweet treat low in sugar and contains protein and more fiber
- Dark chocolate
- A healthy granola bar
- Sea salt crackers and peanut butter
- Beet crystals
- Frozen grapes
- Raw, organic honey
- Vanilla Chai tea

How can I end sugar cravings for good?

Consuming too much sugar and processed foods can create a vicious cycle encouraged by a sugar addiction. Try boosting your serotonin levels. Naturally raise levels of this "happiness hormone" by doing exercise, getting enough sleep, and following a healthy diet.

Greater serotonin levels will lead to less sugar cravings. You can satisfy your sweet tooth naturally with raw organic foods.

What are the symptoms of sugar addiction?

Sugar is often linked to obesity, high blood pressure, hypertension, fatigue, depression and headaches. However, most people may not even realize that they have a problem.

Here are the top five signs that you might be addicted to sugar:

- Overeating on sugary foods more than you intended
- You often crave for or dream about what sugary foods to eat next!
- You eat sugary foods, even when you do not want to eat it
- You eat sugary foods to the point of feeling ill

- You sometimes crave salty foods or meat

What kind of sugar can I cut down on?

You can start to stop or reduce on eating anything with added sugar such as cakes, ice cream, biscuits, yoghurt, chocolate, and also sweetened breakfast cereal. Do not add sugar to your tea or coffee, or drink sugary soft drinks.

What are the different ways I can cut down on sugar?

If you cannot reduce or eliminate sugar completely at first, think about your mindset and what are the sweet things that you can eat instead of added sugar? Some people find using stevia and Xylitol helpful when baking, and they make their sweet snacks and treats using dates or raisins as the sweet ingredient instead of using sugar. Try ripe bananas and cooked sweet potatoes for baking, they can be amazing ingredients. They taste so sweet that no added sugar is required.

What changes do you notice to health when cutting down on sugar?

- After reducing your sugar intake, you may notice that you never feel sleepy in the afternoons, which is wonderful if you have afternoon meetings at work.
- You can exercise without any extreme drops in blood sugar levels.
- You feel less bloated
- Your stomach feels and looks flatter than it's been in years.
- You can enjoy main meals without thinking about having a dessert.
- You no longer constantly think about sweets.
- There are no more overwhelming cravings.

- You begin to feel more in control of your life, and in general you feel much healthier than you did in your teens or 20s.

About the Author

Anthea Peries BSc (Hons) is a published author, she completed her undergraduate studies in several branches of the sciences, including Biology, Brain and Behaviour and Child Development. A former graduate member of the British Psychological Society, she has experience in counselling and is a former senior management executive. Born in London, Anthea enjoys fine cuisine, writing, and has travelled the world.

Thank you for purchasing this book, if you found it helpful, please leave an *honest review* when convenient, on Amazon.

Other Books by This Author

- Food Addiction: Why You Eat to Fall Asleep and How to Overcome Night Eating Syndrome

- Food Addiction: Overcoming Your Addiction to Sugar, Junk Food, and Binge Eating

- Food Addiction: Overcome Sugar Bingeing, Overeating on Junk Food & Night Eating Syndrome

- Food Addiction: Binge Eating Disorders

- Food Addiction: Stop Binge Eating, Food Cravings and Night Eating, Overcome Your

Addiction to Junk Food &
Sugar

- Food Cravings: Simple
  Strategies to Help Deal with
  Craving for Sugar & Junk
  Food

- Overcome Food Addiction:
  How to Overcome Food
  Addiction, Binge Eating and
  Food Cravings

Made in the USA
Las Vegas, NV
09 November 2021